HANDS—ON JOBS

ZOO WORKERS

RICHARD ALEXANDER

PowerKiDS press™

New York

Published in 2016 by The Rosen Publishing Group, Inc.
29 East 21st Street, New York, NY 10010

Copyright © 2016 by The Rosen Publishing Group, Inc.

First Edition

Editor: Katie Kawa
Book Design: Reann Nye

Photo Credits: Cover, pp. 3–24 (background texture) Toluk/Shutterstock.com; cover, p. 13 belizar/Shutterstock.com; p. 5 Image Source/Vetta/Getty Images; p. 6 YASUYOSHI CHIBA/AFP/Getty Images; p. 7 Taylor S. Kennedy/ National Geographic/Getty Images; p. 9 (top) ADRIAN DENNIS/AFP/Getty Images; p. 9 (bottom) Igor Kovalchuk/Shutterstock.com; p. 11 (both) Oli Scarff/ Getty Images News/Getty Images; p. 15 Dan Kitwood/Getty Images News/Getty Images; p. 17 (top) Martin Harvey/Photolibrary/Getty Images; p. 17 (bottom) SERGEI GAPON/AFP/Getty Images; p. 18 Sergey Novikov/Shutterstock.com; p. 19 stockphoto mania/Shutterstock.com; p. 20 JACK GUEZ/AFP/Getty Images; p. 21 EvenEzer/Shutterstock.com; p. 22 JUSTIN TALLIS/AFP/Getty Images.

Cataloging-in-Publication Data

Alexander, Richard.
Zoo workers / by Richard Alexander.
p. cm. — (Hands-on jobs)
Includes index.
ISBN 978-1-5081-4375-8 (pbk.)
ISBN 978-1-5081-4376-5 (6-pack)
ISBN 978-1-5081-4377-2 (library binding)
1. Zoo keepers — Juvenile literature. 2. Zoo keepers — Vocational guidance — Juvenile literature. 3. Zoos — Vocational guidance — Juvenile literature. I. Alexander, Richard. II. Title.
QL50.5 A44 2016
636.088'9'023—d23

Manufactured in the United States of America

CPSIA Compliance Information: Batch #BW16PK: For Further Information contact Rosen Publishing, New York, New York at 1-800-237-9932

CONTENTS

A Wild Job! 4

Doing the Dirty Work 6

New Experiences 8

Helpful Training 10

Special Skills and Qualities. 12

Strong and Safe. 14

Studying Science 16

Hands-On Experience. .18

Other Zoo Workers 20

Worth the Hard Work 22

Glossary 23

Index 24

Websites 24

A WILD JOB!

Imagine having a job that lets you work with animals all day. You would feed them, clean their **habitats**, train them, and even play with them. Does that sound like fun? If it does, then you might want to be a zoo worker when you grow up!

Zoo workers can have many different jobs. Some of them work with animals, and some don't. The workers who provide everyday care for zoo animals are called keepers. A career as a keeper isn't always easy, but it's rewarding to care for the beautiful animals that live in zoos.

DIGGING DEEPER

An aquarium is like a zoo for sea creatures. Keepers who work at an aquarium are often called aquarists.

If you like visiting the zoo and learning about the wild animals that live there, then a career as a zoo worker might be a great fit for you. It's a wild job—and an important one!

DOING THE DIRTY WORK

Zoo workers—especially keepers—can't be afraid to get their hands dirty. It's a keeper's job to clean the habitats of the wild animals that live in zoos. This means doing the dirty work around zoos, such as cleaning up animal waste. It can be a smelly job, but someone has to do it!

Keepers also feed zoo animals. Keepers must know which foods each animal needs to eat. Animals don't all eat the same thing! For some animals, this means giving them **bales** of hay or bunches of fruits and vegetables. For others, this means feeding them raw meat.

DIGGING DEEPER

Zoo workers sometimes feed animals a kind of ice pop made out of their favorite food, such as fruit or meat. This frozen food is something different for an animal to eat. It's important for zoo workers to add as much **variety** to an animal's life as they can.

Zoo workers keep zoo animals healthy by keeping their habitats—and the animals themselves—clean and giving them the right amount of food to eat.

NEW EXPERIENCES

Another important part of a keeper's job is providing zoo animals with different kinds of enrichment. Wild animals have endless opportunities to discover new things. Zoo animals, however, have more limited opportunities for learning and playing. Enrichment is a way for keepers to give zoo animals new things to see, **experience**, and play with.

For example, keepers can put new objects into zoo animals' habitats. These include balls, boxes, and branches. Keepers are always looking for new ways to help zoo animals learn and **explore** the world around them. They study the animals to plan the right enrichment opportunities for them.

DIGGING DEEPER

Introducing animals to new scents is another kind of enrichment used by keepers. One way to do this is by putting different perfume samples in an animal's habitat for them to smell.

Enrichment makes life more exciting and fun for zoo animals, and it can also do the same for keepers.

9

HELPFUL TRAINING

Keepers also train zoo animals. When people think of training animals, they often think of teaching animals tricks for fun. What keepers do with zoo animals, though, is more important than just showing off what animals can learn.

Keepers train animals in order to allow the zoo's **veterinarians** to examine these animals in a way that's safe and comfortable. Keepers train animals to stand on a scale to be weighed. They also train animals to show different body parts without a person touching them. This makes it easier for veterinarians to give an animal the care it needs to stay healthy.

DIGGING DEEPER

Becoming a zoo veterinarian is a great career choice for someone who wants to help animals that are sick. You have to take special college classes in veterinary science to become a zoo veterinarian.

Keepers and veterinarians work together to keep zoo animals healthy. Keepers often work under the **supervision** of veterinarians to give animals medicine and to measure an animal's height and weight, as shown here.

SPECIAL SKILLS AND QUALITIES

Because keepers and other zoo workers such as veterinarians spend so much time around animals, they need to have a special set of skills and qualities to do their job well. Most importantly, they must be good with animals and like being around them. They must also be **patient** and open-minded, because animals can take a long time to train.

Zoo workers also spend a lot of their time talking to people. They often teach people about the animals they work with. For this reason, zoo workers should have strong public speaking skills.

DIGGING DEEPER

Zoo workers often have to take notes about the animals they work with. They need strong writing skills, and they need to be good at noticing details in order to make sure an animal is healthy.

Keepers and veterinarians sometimes care for baby animals. They need to be gentle with these babies in order to give them the care they need.

STRONG AND SAFE

Keepers need to have a certain kind of **personality** in order to be successful. They also need to be strong. They often have to lift heavy things to feed zoo animals or clean their habitats. They must be able to work outside in any kind of weather—from summer heat to winter snow. Keepers don't get to take rainy days off!

Safety is very important for all zoo workers and the animals they care for. Even though zoo animals might look cute and friendly, many of them could be deadly if approached by someone without proper training.

DIGGING DEEPER

Zoo workers have a higher chance of getting hurt or sick at work than the average American worker.

Keepers often work long hours, but their love of animals helps them enjoy the hard work they're doing.

STUDYING SCIENCE

Keepers need to learn as much as they can about animals before they start working with them. If you want to be a keeper someday, you'll need to take as many science classes as possible. It's also helpful to have good math skills. Many of the notes taken by keepers are numbers, such as animals' weights and the amount of food they eat.

Getting a four-year college degree is important if you want to be a keeper. Keepers generally study science in college. Common branches of science they study include biology, which is the study of living things, and animal **behavior**.

DIGGING DEEPER

Some zoo workers study zoology in college. Zoology is a branch of biology that deals only with animals.

You can learn more about what it takes to become a zoo worker by talking to one. The next time you go to a zoo, ask one of the keepers about how they got their job and what a day at work is like for them.

HANDS-ON EXPERIENCE

Taking the right science and math classes is only part of what you'll need to do if you want to become a zoo worker. The other part is working with animals. An **internship** at a zoo during college is a great step toward a career as a zoo worker.

There are also things you can do long before college to gain experience working with animals. **Volunteering** at a zoo, aquarium, or local animal shelter is a great place to start. If you live on a farm that raises animals, you already have valuable animal experience!

DIGGING DEEPER

Walking dogs around your neighborhood is another good way to gain experience working with animals. You can also practice being a keeper by taking care of your own pets, including feeding them and cleaning up after them.

Volunteering at a zoo or animal shelter does much more than provide experience for a future career. It allows you to make a difference in the lives of animals that need our help.

OTHER ZOO WORKERS

Most people think of a career as a keeper when they imagine working at a zoo. However, many other jobs are open to people who want to work at a zoo but don't want to be a keeper.

If you want a career that combines medicine and zoo animals, then you might be interested in a career as a veterinarian at a zoo. If you like working with people and animals, you might make a good volunteer coordinator. This person is in charge of all the volunteers at a zoo.

DIGGING DEEPER

Another zoo worker who uses medicine to help zoo animals is a veterinary technician. This is a person who helps a zoo's veterinarian and works under them to provide medical care for a zoo's animals.

JOBS AT A ZOO

KEEPER
provides basic care for animals

VETERINARIAN
provides medical care for animals

VOLUNTEER COORDINATOR
is in charge of zoo volunteers

VETERINARY TECHNICIAN
helps the veterinarian

GENERAL CURATOR
is in charge of a zoo's entire animal collection

CURATOR OF EDUCATION
plans zoo's educational programs

DEVELOPMENT DIRECTOR
leads efforts to raise money for a zoo

DIRECTOR OF CONSERVATION
is in charge of a zoo's conservation efforts, or efforts to keep wild animals safe

These are just some of the many careers you can choose from if you want to work at a zoo.

WORTH THE HARD WORK

Zoo workers have chosen a career that allows them to spend time around some of the most amazing wild animals on Earth—from powerful lions to cute penguins. However, their job isn't all fun and games. They work very hard to make sure these animals are fed, are healthy, and have a clean place to live.

The next time you visit a zoo, pay attention to the people working alongside the animals. If you work and study hard enough, you could find yourself in this wild career field one day, caring for some of our planet's coolest animals!

GLOSSARY

bale: A large, tight group of objects tied together.

behavior: The way a person or animal acts.

experience: Skill or knowledge you get by doing something. Also, to do or see something.

explore: To search something to find out more about it.

habitat: The place where an animal lives or grows.

internship: A job done—often without pay—in order to gain experience.

patient: Able to remain calm when waiting for a long time or dealing with problems.

personality: The set of qualities and ways of behaving that make a person different from other people.

supervision: The act of watching and directing what someone does or how something is done.

variety: The state of having many different things.

veterinarian: An animal doctor.

volunteer: To do something to help because you want to do it and not for pay.

INDEX

A
animal behavior, 16
aquarists, 4
aquarium, 4, 18

B
biology, 16

C
cleaning, 4, 6, 14, 18
college, 10, 16, 18

E
enrichment, 8, 9

F
feeding, 4, 6, 14, 18

I
internships, 18

K
keepers, 4, 6, 8, 9, 10, 11,
    12, 13, 14, 15, 16,
    17, 18, 20, 21

M
math, 16, 18

P
public speaking, 12

S
scents, 8
science, 10, 16, 18
skills, 12, 16

T
training, 4, 10, 12, 14

V
veterinarians, 10, 11, 12, 13,
    20, 21
volunteer, 18, 19, 20, 21

WEBSITES

Due to the changing nature of Internet links, PowerKids Press has developed an online list of websites related to the subject of this book. This site is updated regularly. Please use this link to access the list: www.powerkidslinks.com/hoj/zoo